High Sea Watch

Ohryong Kwon

BookLeaf Publishing

India | USA | UK

Presentation by *BookLeaf Publishing*

Web: www.bookleafpub.com

E-mail: info@bookleafpub.com

ISBN: 978-93-5744-884-0

First edition 2022

PREFACE

Because every misery

has its own rhythm within

Fall 2021

Ohryong Kwon

Pupil dives

After a dance forever. we drop to the floor
Forgiveness all ready

Now how can I return home?
Cause the equator's swarming with your traitors

Nile Blue

Night?
Night.

I pleaded till I turned pale.

As if I knew those praying hands. They say I
limped for all my life
Had no reason nor need to leave: stood frozen
with a grin: compliant and sweet

decrescendo
It was here and now it's gone
Four-four time repeated for ever

Saw a man in tantrum I stole his bike
Cause condolers need no leg
I've learned that from church while wagging my
tail

and then came nothing
"Nile", said it

Sentential Logic Practice

-prove the argument invalid

[Premise 1]
There was a mirror in her room
She wasn't there. The mirror was there

[Premise 2]
Cut off the temples of a saint
But Mom. He hit me first

[Premise 3]
I throw myself out the balcony and shout
: artist, if talkative, is sin

[Premise 4]
Now home is a thousand and six hundred
kilometers away
People wept like sirens during dawns
Our bodies like pendulums
if we could call this eternity

[Conclusion]

Snatching blossoms

I'll be on your side

Night is one pattern of love. My only aim was chastity If my fate was to be ruined, but really, where did he disappear? Nobody practiced my facial expressions. If only I could make this my best last free fall

Clocks that stopped yesterday, adieu

Clown nose

I believe in shoes
But they're trembling: my
Lips. My lips
Won't you believe?

Have always been alone on stage
They pay me for mockery
and the Audience: laughs to the beat
Hilarious? Think that's funny? Professor.

I wanted to be you. Stepping to the music, I
wanted to be you. Singing something obvious, I
wanted to betray you
And yes it is hard to breathe. wearing fake
noses, I practiced this since yesterday 내가
한국어로 말하면 왜 다들 웃지요?

I believe in clowns
But rattle rattle
trembles: my voice. Voice
Can you believe?

Somnipathy

Heard that Summer passed away
Was burning petals for four days
Slowly I swallow (Today's the second day)

Mommy says she isn't well – we got her
bleached for every day
"Shall we cut our both hands off?"
I sat and stared: no age was too young for
obituary

At nights with crevices would old lovers arrive
"You forgot our chansons, how could you? how
would you
My low and clandestine, you, how could you
(thought my name was salvation)
Banish the gaps: be broken yet beautiful
I watch your movies to watch you make lies"
(knew not the pages we spent was blasphemy)

Three days passed cause summer was dead
Wind blew fast cause windows were shut

: No name to call.

Mostly Abandoned. but

did you weep
?

17 Daehak-ro 10 gil

(Teach me:
What face do I make for curtain calls?)

World's sloppiest two person play
When all stage lights are off
We enough, love, henceforth towards the brick
red abyss

Glittering shimmering cutesy-poo cookie doughs

I'll have to confess.
I've done something
and the something went wrong

I say "My bad." to make my lips look pretty
and Therefore you feel pity for me
Pious men are crazy for me
Say hello to your lover: that's me, your lover,
the submissive, beloved; detested, and beloved.
That's me; the worst thing that happened to you;
that's you

Chime bells from vacation-church-schools
I major ballet to leave you on tiptoes
Do you like this? liked that? you find this
enjoyable?
If Pow pow! then all turns warm

But Worry not!
For Even our deathbed looks so cute

10

Fiasco

3 seconds of embrace
Clarification 60 full seconds
Things that flew away to unlearn
Last page was missing in the first place
, Love the useless me,
It's all you outside of me
Outside my solitude is your torment
Let's not trust it
let's not overflow

Let's overflow

Your name your summer your sole your habits,
exhalation, Blue flowers on an improper branch
Our fall. our soul
Fiasco

Theory of forgiveness

Hated you for coming up in my mind Not your
fault but Have I gone out of my mind? Have
been deboning addressless thoughts of mine If
only a piece of it could reach you afar If only I
could break you down towards my side

When you, the last year's person, called me late
night I held my breath twice before I pick up the
phone Oblivion has always been my chronics so
that is why I practiced my hatred I'll never like
you carelessly I'd never

Done with your business you scatter like some
offensive joke and I left alone Putting down the
phone the whole world seems dead I tried my
best to go back into sleep for my mind kept
running out the window Loving you meant
loving even my own stupidity Even though I
was all aware I hear wind coming out from my
bosom You always came back naming my dearth
and I've always wished I could drown myself
near you

Killing tides

How would I possibly abandon you
     A reply to this requires a drowning
The tides hit for three hours only, This low
     pitched night, and you're always, fuck, like
this. We still a cliché and an unnamed sea
     Few couples that just drifted away
The very last ebb of my life and
     How could you possibly abandon me

Ritual

But I have a wife.

About the endless requiem
About the face which exhausted its lies

Hid my thoughts within the spacings
people here don't know me quite
I wanna be famous. I'm gonna be famous
Search my name everyday on Google. I gotta be
famous

VOA visited to interview me yesterday.
Beating the. Beating the shit out of her. I can do
that. Beating is my specialty
Only when I beat I forget to stutter

Every kiss requires the bending of my back
Let's meet no more.
My girl already blind

: (with eyes wide
open)

But
Socrates.
Why not dead yet?

Still-life

Inside it's empty
Flip over then stab; blue blood'll come out
Tranquility of a stray satellite
That cosmic desolation

It's quiet. silent
For my god does not speak in English

Injured little yellow saucer, all tissues used for
blowing our nose, walked-over oral angles,
Harsh scolding, Thigh muscles, worst corner of
the wall, oxford commas.
… I wanted you
Today we break away with a torn bible in our
hands

Unhappy percussions

My darling ain't dead; she fell. That's what I
was told. Your father was hiding his hands
behind me (was he tapdancing internally?)

Look. I've decided to wobble no more. That's
why I learned philosophy; I hate nausea and you
know that. Wobbling taught me that all good
philosophers were dead already so now you join
that side, while we were fooling around, I hoped
you'd walk slightly just a little bit slower and
Could you please stop laughing

Entering a small room I see your face. Silly
smile on that photo. It's only you, flowerbed,
and the others are weeping. I crawled towards
you – had something desperate to tell her

I collapse in offbeat every day, this is my
habitual downfall, I kept be broken offbeat
Everybody but you here speaks with their butt
Instead of saying I miss you I'll say I'll forget

Overgrown embryos cry next door. I looked up
to check you: only you still smiling

18

Wave height 16

My mind lingers where the tides had left
So done with this plunge Was the teacher's pet
since forty-one
Tie a price tag to god's ankle
This I call the city's dignity. I pray

And you're not a poem: your face. Your vocal.
My three years.
Promise. I'll never dance again.
speechless, I crumple my heels

(pondering for four seconds
: the sea won't cease
Under sands, knees sleep deep)

After all we're not a play
I bury you to break away
love
weren't we better yesterday

Understudy

My people with stolen faces My people, my people lie down on bed Walk on colorless streets Earn as much trouble as money While liking my post on Instagram though they not "like" it Run after others just like the others Become new others to the others Don't quite know but either laugh or yell like those others Endures life like a loaded bus Could not overcome yet could neither suicide Those already dead –"And really this'll be the last time"-, be deceived once more. to crawl back into our mothers' wombs

If end of life was death could end of death be life Among spotless inquiries buildings with machines dance in circles Can hear prayers in foreign languages Trees are all stiffened The dead sneak peek at the yet-to-dies Seasons fool us then scatter into a thousand, a thousand Outside the window came the plague They told me about your risk Tomorrow your pot will boil again So no one cares about poetry I mean who cares

Apostate

21

There was a girl who had a strange name
People stall before they call my name

Very likely that I've lost my mind
As if begging I still come back

Jan's room

No we could not help it
I was the one who hugged you first Didn't know
where else to put myself
I know. We were desperate. dark and young,
weren't we heavy equally
It's a bit dirty but would you mind? Our
summer. Your semi-basement
It was the director's subplot. Didn't we know at
least better than the others?

My shitty bashfulness. Haven't even removed
my lips
Since when did ant colonies march around your
place?
I pressed it. grab then kill. Look how obedient
and quiet I am
You love it when I do this, right?
didn't you find my ruthlessness "adorable"

Jan, your last year's house so far and dim
Jan, my Jan, now lying alone to blubber blubber
No hope and we went too far. sorry.
Expansions between us will last: forever

October's innocence

Tautly kissing
like a bowstring
Pull and release: you find nothing. Like music?
Like music
Afar yet the sea repeats for a thousand time
and You say that you'd never had me right

There are no lines in this film
Like void.
Like fragment

If it's not my will to beat my pulse
Thou. we only have our farewell left

20211021

24

Spring was not my fault. My agony 19 stories
high; I get skewed for I cannot be deeper. Hates
weather forecasts. Wanted to be cheery but
couldn't help. G minor. This is nobody's song. I
claim

Learning that everything was my fault, I kissed
the void to erase myriads

Twentytwo was its name. Twenty two.